SUFI LOVE POETRY

By the same author:

Poetry of Light: Sufi Poetry from Persia, 2007

The author is grateful to Gail Larrick, Rudite Emir, Debra Mcdonald, and Farideh Rasti for editing; Farzaneh Rasti for calligraphy; and Fabrizio Pregadio for helping to bring the book to publication.

Sufi Love Poetry

Rumi and Other Masters
and Poets of Persia

Translated from the original Persian
by Parviz N. Rasti

Sufi Cultural Center & Coffee Shop
Mountain View, California

© 2011 by Parviz N. Rasti

ISBN 978-0-9847358-7-7 (pbk)

Photos by Parviz N. Rasti

Sufi Cultural Center & Coffee Shop
815 West El Camino Real
Mountain View, CA 94040
www.suficoffeeshop.org
suficulturalcenter@gmail.com

Printed in the United States of America

Typeset in Sabon

Contents

Dedication, vii

"The World of Love and Intoxication,"
  by Dr. Javad Nurbakhsh, 1

"Remembering the Master,"
  by Parviz N. Rasti, 3

Hafez, 5

Shah Ni'matullah, 41

Rumi, 53

Sa'di, 87

Biographies of the Poets, 97

Notes, 107

  Sufi Symbolism, 109

  Notes to Poems, 112

In the Name of the Beloved,

this book is dedicated to

Master Dr. Javad Nurbakhsh

(1926–2008)

and

Present Master Dr. Alireza Nurbakhsh

The World of Love and Intoxication

by Dr. Javad Nurbakhsh

The world of love and intoxication has neither peace nor
    security.
Its pain, sorrow, and affliction make neither sigh nor wailing.

Such an astonishing dimension! It is out of both worlds.
It is beyond space and time with no borders and frontiers.

In that domain, there is no mention of you or me.
There is no intelligence nor knowledge. It has no
    explanation.

Whoever becomes His acquaintance is a stranger to himself.
Wherever that one goes, he is alone, has no trace or name.

The one, free from everything, has no news of oneself.
Thoughts of being and nonbeing have nothing but harm.

The crazy[1] one on His path is said to have Divine Wisdom.
Although he is the dearest, he has no fear of losing his life.

Since Nurbakhsh sincerely gambled everything in the lane of
    love,
he no longer expects any assistance from this one and that
    one.

Remembering the Master, Dr. Javad Nurbakhsh

by Parviz N. Rasti

October is the cruelest month.
Today is an April day.
Until I see you again,
I will remain in my dreams
with your glance of a thousand rays
bestowing light.

You stand
on a cliff
in front of an unfinished Sufi house
as we help dig a cave
and roll away boulders.
Thousands of years of history are being replaced,
condensed into a few months.

Hot and hazy red and yellow horizon.
After a long, frenzied, happy day of work,
we retreat for a cup of delightful evening tea
and wait for your rapturous laughter.
You say,
This world is not even a drop before the ocean of love.

Years and years later,
twenty-two years—
it seems just a moment has passed—
I see you again.
The joy of an April day.

October is the cruelest month.
You are not among us anymore.
I will remain in my dreams,
longing for your rapturous laughter.

HAFEZ

The Master of the Holy Fire

As long as a trace and a name remain from the Wine and
    Tavern,
my head will be on the dust of the path of the Master of the
    Holy Fire.[2]

From the beginning, the ring of His Love has pierced my ear.
I remain what I was and will be the same at the end.

When you pass by my gravestone, ask for aspiration,
for this stone will be a shrine of pilgrimage for the *rendan*.[3]

Be quiet, O you self-centered ascetic, from your eyes and
    mine
the secret has remained hidden and will be a mystery.

My merciless, intoxicated Beloved went out today,
so Her beauty brings forth tears of blood from everyone's
    eyes.

The moment my head rests joyously in the grave, my eyes
will anxiously await the dawn of resurrection to open again.

If the fortune of Hafez is helping him like this, it seems
the tresses of the Beloved will be in the hands of others.

On the Threshold

I have the decree of the Master of the Holy Fire—an old
saying:
Wine is forbidden where the Beloved is not present.

I rend apart this garb of hypocrisy. What am I to do?
The soul suffers greatly conversing with the wrong ones.

Hoping for a sip of wine from the lips of the Soul of souls,
for years I have remained at the Tavern's threshold, waiting.

He hasn't forgotten my service of long ago, has He?
O breeze of dawn, remind Him of the time past.

If You pass over my grave after a hundred years,
my decayed bones will rise up from my clay, dancing.

The Beloved first takes my heart with a hundred promises.
It seems the Fair-tempered One will not forget His old
pledge.

O blossom, don't be broken-hearted about the unlucky
fortune:
You will be helped by the breath of early morning and the
breeze.

O heart, thinking to heal yourself is a futile effort.
The heartache of a lover will not be cured by a healer.

Learn the gem of esoteric knowledge, which you can take
    with you,
for the others have silver and gold for their lot of fate.

The snares are difficult unless the Grace of God helps,
for no human is spared by the damned Satan.

O Hafez, if you do not possess silver and gold, don't fret.
    Thank God.
What is better than the blessing of eloquent speech and
    inspired heart?

People of the Heart

When you hear the people of the heart speak, don't say they
  are wrong.
You don't recognize eloquent speech, my dear. That is what
  is wrong.

I will not bow down my head before the worlds of here and
  hereafter.
Glory be to God for all these conspiracies in our mind.

I do not know who is inside my weary heart.
I am silent, but he is wailing with commotion.

Where are You, O Minstrel? My heart tore this veil apart.
Sing a song. Your songs bring happiness and calm.

I never paid any attention to worldly affairs.
It was Your beautiful face that made them so wondrous.

I haven't slept because of a thought that my heart is weaving.
I have a hundred nights of craving. Where is the Tavern of
  Wine?

Now that the monastery became sullied by my heart's blood,
if You wash and cleanse me with wine, You are justified.

The reason that I am so dear to the Temple of the Holy Fire
is that the fire that never dies will forever be in my heart.

What scale did the Minstrel play behind the veil?
My life is gone, yet my head is still filled with desires.

Your call of love resonated deep in my heart last night.
The space in Hafez's heart is still filled with sound.

The Secret

For any seeker who found the path to the Tavern,
to knock on any other door is sheer futility.

Whoever found a way to the threshold of the Tavern
earned *khaniqah*'s[4] secret from the grace of the wine.

Life didn't bestow the crown of *rendi*[5] except on the one
who exalted this honor above all other things in life.

Ask for nothing beyond the devotion of the crazy[6] ones,
for the sheikhs[7] of our path considered sanity as sin.

Whoever read the secret of both worlds in the grooves of the
    Cup
earned the mystery of Jamshid's goblet[8] from traces of the
    dust of the path.

My heart did not ask forgiveness from the *Saqi*'s[9] eyes,
for it knew the crafty ways of the hard-hearted Beloved.

From the suffering of the lot of my fortune's star, at dawn,
my eyes cried so much that Venus saw and the Moon
    understood.

Happy the sight that sees the cup's curve and the *Saqi*'s face,
as the new moon's curve and the full moon's beauty on the
    fourteenth night.

In secret they talk about Hafez and his wine-drinking. Let it
    be!
There is no place for religious clerics and judges. The King
    knows it all.

Praise the highest King that the nine magnificent heavens
are but a mere arch in His courtly hall of majesty.

Don't Part from Me

Don't part from me, for You are the light of my eyes,
calming the soul, and the companion of my trembling heart.

Lovers will not cease imploring You for Your love.
You have torn away their garb of patience.

May Your good fortune be safe, free from the evil eye,
for You have reached the ultimate in stealing the heart.

O lofty ascetic, do not prevent my loving Him.
Since you haven't seen Him, you will be excused.

O Hafez, I wonder why the Friend scolded you.
You haven't stepped up and crossed your line, have you?

رهرو منزل عشقیم و ز سرحد عدم
تا به اقلیم وجود این همه راه آمده ایم

لنگر حلم تو ای کشتی توفیق کجاست
که درین بحر کرم غرق گناه آمده ایم

تا مگر جرعه فشاند لب جانان بر من
سالها شد که منم بر در میخانه مقیم

بعد صد سال اگر بر سر خاکم گذری
سر برآرد ز گلم رقص کنان عظم رمیم

I Kiss Her Lips

I kiss Her lips and drink the wine.
I have found the life-giving water.

Neither can I tell anyone about this mystery,
nor can I bear to see anyone with Her.

The goblet kisses Her lips and suffers in vain.
The flower sees Her face and sweats with shame.

Give me a cup of wine, do not recall King Jam.[10]
Who knows who Jam was and when was Kay?[11]

Strike the harp in secret, O moon minstrel.
Strike its veins so they gush forth in pain.

The flower brought forth news from Her retreat.
As the bud journeys, leave asceticism aside and bloom.

Like Her eyes, don't let the drunken one languish.
Her red lips! O cupbearer, pour more wine!

The soul does not want to be apart from that beautiful form,
for it has Her goblet of blood in its marrow and veins.

O Hafez, hold back your tongue for the time being.
Hearken to the reed of those without tongues.

Never Quit Drinking Wine

I will never quit drinking wine in the flower season.
I brag about being rational, but never practice it.

Where is the minstrel to spend all that's been earned
from knowledge to piety on songs of the reed and playing
    the lute, the harp?

My heart aches from the uproar and hubbub of learning.
Now it is time to be of service to the Beloved, and wine.

When was there fidelity in any age? O bring me a cup of
    wine!
How long should I talk about King Jam and Kavous the
    Great?[12]

I am not afraid to be recorded on the blacklist at
    Resurrection,
for through His grace hundreds of blacklists will be
    obsolete.

Where is the morning messenger, that ultimate auspicious
    fortune,
in whom to confide my suffering of the night of separation?

This borrowed life the Friend bestowed upon Hafez.
I will, one day when I behold His Face, surrender to Him.

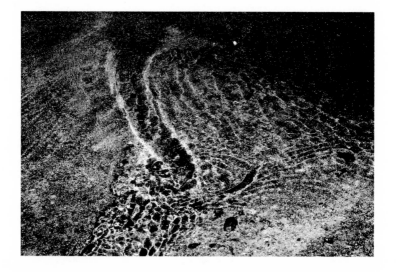

The Jewels of the Hidden Mysteries

The jewels of the hidden mysteries are the same as they were.
The chalice of loving still carries the signs and traces—as it
   did.

The lovers are among the chosen trusted ones.
Thus the eyes are full of precious drops—as they were.

Ask the zephyr whether every night until the edge of dawn
the aroma of Your tresses will be the companion of the
   soul—as it was.

The Sun is not after precious stones and brilliant rubies
after creating the troves and the mines—as it did.

Come! Have pity on the one who is dying for one glance,
for the wretched one's heart is still aching—as it was.

The color of my heart's blood that You are hiding
was revealed by Your ruby-colored lips—as they did.

I thought Your pitch-black tresses would not beguile me.
Years passed by and they are still doing the same—as they
   did.

O Hafez! Tell us about your yearning, burning tears,
and tears are still flowing from this spring—as they were.

The Clay of Adam

Last night I saw angels knocking on the Tavern door.
They were kneading the clay of Adam, blending it with
    wine.

Those who live in the impeccable sanctuary of Heaven
drank a cupful of spirits with this drunken wayfarer.

Heaven and Earth could not bear the trust of Love,
so the honor was bestowed on this poor, crazy soul.

Excuse the war among all nations and cultures.
Not seeing the truth, they made up fables, tales instead.

Thank God, peace prevailed between Him and me.
Grateful, the Sufis began to dance, drinking wine.

That is not the fire with which the flame of a candle flutters.
It is the fire that consumed the moth completely.

No one before Hafez lifted the veils from the face of
    thought,
since the tresses of eloquent speech were combed with pens.

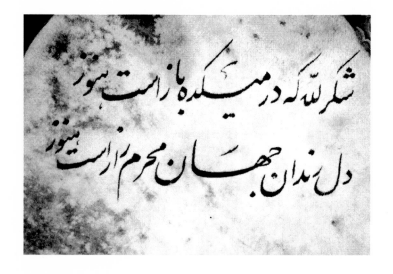

Last Night, at Dawn

Last night, at dawn, I was relieved of my sorrow.
In the midst of darkness, I was given the life-giving water.

I went beyond myself in the radiance of His Essence.
I was given wine from the splendid goblet of Eternal
   Attribute.

What an auspicious night and blessed dawn!
Fortune descended during the Night of nights.

Now, the mirror of His beauty and my face
bring forth tidings of the manifestation of the Essence.

If I have become fortunate, with a heart filled with joy,
it is because I was given the alms that I deserved.

From the unseen, I was given the good news of this fortune,
for I bore suffering with patience and constancy.

All this sweetness and eloquence in my poetry
are the reward for my patience, from the source of sweetness.

It was Hafez's aspiration and the help of those early risers
that released him from the bond of the sorrow of life.

If I Go from This Ruined House

If I go from this ruined house toward home,
when I reach there, I promise to be wise and sane.

If from this trip I make it home safe and sound,
I will make a pledge to head directly to the Tavern.

I'll tell what I discovered from my journey and seeking.
I will go to the Sanctuary door with wine, playing the lute.

If those on the path of Love shed my blood,
curses be on me if I turn to a stranger and gripe.

From now on, with my hands and the chains of the Beloved's
    tresses,
I'll keep following the desire of my crazy heart.

If once more I behold the Beloved's eyebrow like an altar,
I will humbly bow down, offering my thanks in gratitude.

Happy is the moment when Hafez, with the help of the
    vizier,
joyfully goes Home from the Tavern with the Friend.

Yearning for Your Lips

My heart and soul keep craving for Your ruby lips,
hoping to sip from the cup of Your beauty, still drinking
    dregs.

On the first day, Your tresses consumed my faith.
With You in my heart, what will become of me at the end?

O Cupbearer, give me a sip of that fiery wine,
for among Her consummated lovers, I am still raw.

I called Your tresses *Chinese musk* by mistake.
Each moment, I still feel stung, remembering it.

The Sun saw a ray of Your face in my retreat with You,
and it still lurks around my roof and door as shade.

Once the Beloved unintentionally mentioned my name.
The people of the heart still feel the aroma of Love from my
    name.

In the beginning, the Cupbearer of Your ruby lips
gave me a sip from Your cup. I haven't gotten sober yet.

You said, *Give up your life so your heart will be calm.*
I gave up my soul for Her sake—yet I am still not calm.

With his pen, Hafez wrote about Her beautiful rubylike lips.
Every moment, Life-giving water pours forth from every pen
     I hold.

Through His Aloofness

Through His aloofness, He turned me into dust on the path.
I kiss the dust under His feet, contrite at being mere dust.

God forbid if I should moan that You have given me a hard
     time.
I am a faithful servant and a devotee of Your court.

I have tied my longing hopes to Your curled tresses.
Let it not be seen that the hand of my seeking seeks less.

I am a particle of dust, happy to be dwelling in Your lane,
fearful that a sudden wind may blow me away, O my Friend.

At dawn, the Master of the Tavern gave me a world-revealing
     goblet.
I witnessed Your beauty in that mirrorlike cup.

I am a Sufi from the temple of the Immaculate Domain.
Now, for the time being, the Tavern of the Holy Fire is my
     lot.

Come with this wayfarer and travel to the Tavern
to see how lofty is my place in that circle.

You passed by drunk without paying attention to Your
     Hafez.
O beware! His sigh may touch the expanse of Your beauty.

What joy at dawn when the King of the East declared:
With all my kingliness, I am the servant of the Tooran king.[13]

I Am the One

I am the one who is famous and crazy about loving.
I am the one who hasn't polluted the eyes by beholding evil,

being loyal, bearing blame with a joyful heart,
for, on our path, to be offended is unfaithfulness.

I asked the Master of the Tavern how to be liberated.
He asked for a cup of wine and said, *Overlook faults.*

What is the purpose of beholding the world's Orchard?
It is to pick the flowers of Your face with the pupils of the
    eyes.

Being intoxicated, I washed my image in running water
to destroy for good the face of my self-worshiping self.

I am so confident of Your benevolent, merciful tresses,
for without Your attraction, all my effort is useless.

I will gallop fast to the Tavern from this assembly.
It is a must to ignore those who preach without practicing.

Learn from the Beloved's face how to be beautiful and
     loving,
to circle happily around the beautiful faces of the ones most
     fair.

O Hafez, kiss only the lips of the Cupbearer and the cup of
     wine.
Be sure to avoid kissing the hand of the pseudo-ascetics.

Don't Brag

I went to the Tavern door, tipsy, last night,
my robe and prayer rug stained with wine.

The wine seller came forward, lamenting,
saying, *O you tipsy wayfarer, wake up!*

Wash yourself and then stroll to the Tavern of Ruin
that this Tavern may not be contaminated by you.

How long will you go after those sweet lips,
tainting the Essence with melting, rubylike desire?

Spend your old age in chastity and do not let
youthfulness contaminate Shoaib's[14] *gift.*

Purify and clean yourself. Emerge from the carnal well.
The earthy, polluted water is not purifying.

I said, *O Universal Mirror: There are no faults with the Book*
     of Creation
when at springtime everything is drunk and intoxicated.

Those on the path of Love in the depth of the sea
were drowned but not touched by the water.

He said, O *Hafez, don't brag about what you know to your*
    friends.
Oh, how lovely is His grace, full of a variety of
    chastisements.

Sound Mind

Anyone who has a sound mind and an adorable beloved
will have prosperity and fortune on his side.

The court of the Sanctuary of Love is higher than the
     intellect.
The one who kisses that threshold holds his life in his hands.

Is Her small, sweet mouth the domain of Solomon?
The design on Her ruby signet has the whole world under its
     charm.

The ruby lips and the black eyebrows—she has both these
     and those.
I am so proud of my beloved, for her beauty has them both.

O prosperous one, do not look down on the meek and the
     weak,
for the highest place of happiness has a beggar on its path.

While on this Earth, cherish your ability as a blessing,
for the era of inability is far beyond your control.

The prayer of the needy ones will turn away affliction from
     body and soul.
Who will benefit from that crop when one is ashamed of the
     pickers?

O Zephyr, tell my fair Beloved the secret of my love—
She, who has among Her least servants hundreds of kings
     like Jam and Khosro.[15]

She may say, *I do not want a lover who is poor, empty-
     handed as Hafez.*
Tell Her, *A Queen needs to have a beggar as a companion.*

It's Enough

O heart, for you, a good companion and a sincere friend are
    enough.
A breeze, heralding from the rose garden of Shiraz, is
    enough.

O Dervish, never take a trip away from the Beloved's side.
A spiritual journey and a corner in the Sufi house are
    enough.

If sorrow ambushes you from the hidden chamber of your
    heart,
you have the Master's threshold as a place of safety—it's
    enough.

Sit at the upper part in an assembly, drink a cup of wine
from the world of prestige and desire. That much is enough.

Don't ask for more. Take the world with ease as it comes.
A cup of rubylike wine, a moon-face Beloved are enough.

The wheel of life fulfills the ignorant people's desires.
You are a person of virtue and knowledge. This sin is
    enough.

Desiring the sweet home and the pledge of the good old
    friend—
the apology of the wayfarers who journeyed home is enough.

Don't get used to being obligated to others, for in both
    worlds
God's contentment and the King's rewards are enough.

O Hafez, there is no need for any other litanies.
A midnight prayer and the morning contemplation are
    enough.

SHAH NI'MATULLAH

A Wave in the Ocean

I will journey to the court of the Tavern of Ruin.
Happily, I will reside in the district of the Holy Fire.

I will travel from the Tavern of Annihilation to subsistence in
    God.
I will abandon myself and become traceless and nameless.

Although I grew old in the Tavern of the Master of the Holy
    Fire,
by the fortune of that Master, I will be young again.

Since nothing but His reflection is engraved on my eyes,
reflecting Him in whatever I see makes me more anxious.

Wherever there was a cup of wine, I cherished it,
as if I'd become the Cupbearer in the world of *rendan*.[16]

I am like a wave that appeared on the surface of the sea.
Come, be my companion for a moment, for soon I'll
    disappear.

Ni'matullah[17] is like a reflection you see in your sleep.
If it is not yet so, within a week I will become one.

ما در انفس و آفاق کسی خوب ندیدیم

در ظاهر و در باطن آثار تو بودیم

I'm Your Cure

The pain of the heart said, *I'm your cure.*
The soul's yearning said, *I'm the Soul of souls.*

The drunken eye said, *I will take your belief away.*
The infidelity of the tresses said, *I am your belief.*

His tresses were disheveled over His face,
saying, *I'm the tranquility of your distressed mind.*

The Master said to one of his needy devotees,
I'm the living treasure in your corner of ruin.

The Minstrel of lovers sings a harmonious song:
The intoxicated nightingale in your flower garden? It is I.

The happy, drunken Cupbearer, with the goblet in His hand,
came over implying, *I'm your guest.*

I told Him, *The Master is the servant of Your love.*
He said, *Yes, of course you are, for I'm your King.*

Making the Old Young Again

O lovers, O lovers, I make the old young again.
O thirsty ones, O thirsty ones, I turn a drop into an ocean.

O seekers, O seekers, I am the oculist in the domain of
    wisdom.
With one glance, I will grant vision to the person born blind.

If the mute one comes to me, I'll glance at him one moment
and make his speech eloquent and sweet like a nightingale's.

If the ego commits a bad deed, I will chastise it promptly,
and if the intellect causes trouble, it will be disgraced at
    once.

I'm a *rend*[18] in the District of Bewilderment, happily drunk
    from the goblet of Unity.
I came to the District of Ruin to ravage the Tavern without
    end.

I'm the moth of His candle, I'm the tranquility at His
    banquet.
I'm the nightingale in the garden crying out to the Highest
    for love of a flower.

A message came from placelessness, O Master of Eternity:
Hide yourself from both worlds,[19] *so then I will show*
    Myself to you.

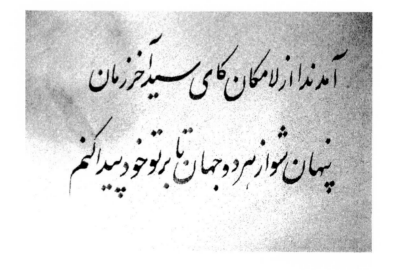

I Saw an Image of His Face

I saw an image of His face in my dream last night.
One could see the moon at night. I saw the Sun.

Wherever the sight fell, I saw just a limitless ocean.
Bright as the light of the eye, I saw a moon in the water.

Every sign that I see is the world-seeing Goblet.
I saw such a beautiful, delicate Cup, full of wine.

For a lifetime, I went through the lane of the Tavern.
I saw the Wine Bearer of the *rendan*[20] banquet, stone drunk.

Whatever shapes I saw became meaningful in Him.
Meaning and shapes were just water and foam.

My I-ness was gone, His He-ness became visible.
I saw Him joyfully through His eyes with no veil.

Now the hidden treasure was revealed to me.
The Secret, which is veiled, I saw with no veil.

From the light of Ni'matullah,[21] the whole world is radiating
    light.
Clearly, I saw His light shining in both the young and the
    old.

At Ease with the World

It is so wonderful to be at ease with the whole world.
To be at ease is good, my dear, if it is just for a moment.

If you want a true companion, take up a cup of wine as I do.
If you are looking for an intimate friend, you are the one.

I am drunk in the tavern. The Cupbearer holds a cup in Her
    hand.
Whoever drinks from the goblet of Jam[22] has news of me.

Visualizing His image and the light radiating from my eyes,
those two are sitting drunk side by side in total solitude.

For those yearning for His love, the dregs of His Pain are the
    cure.
Come and drink some wine so you will be happily drunk at
    once.

Drinking rapturous wine, talking about love — beware
of seeing God in my eyes, and my eyes are His.

Oh, go, you wandering intellect. I am drunk and you are
    languishing.
I am with Ni'matullah,[23] and I am at ease with the whole
    world.

RUMI

RUMI

Like Life

You are going like life secretly into my soul.
You are my strolling Cypress, O the splendor of my
    Orchard!

Don't go without me. Take a body, O the Life of souls.
Don't leave my eyes, O my ever-illuminating torch!

I rend apart the seven heavens, I go beyond the seven seas
when You look with love through my wandering soul.

When You came to my embrace, I enslaved faith and
    disbelief.
Seeing You is my religion and Your face is my belief.

You took away my mind. You made me sleepless with no
    food.
Come to Jacob, O my Joseph, O my Canaan, O my Joseph!

Through Your grace, I became a spirit invisible to myself,
O You, whose Being is hiding in my invisible being.

The Narcissus eye is drunk, the flower's garb torn because of
    You.
You are the water of the branches, O You, my endless
    Orchard!

One moment You brand me, another, You pull me to the
Orchard.
Pull me to the light so that my eyes will open wide.

O Soul before all souls, O Treasure before all treasures,
You are much more than those. You are mine, and You are
mine.

Since my Home is not of clay, I have no fear if my body falls
apart.
My reflection is not upon heaven. Union with You is my
goal.

Remembering Your moon face, alas, my sighs and my grief
remain,
and the aroma of my King, and my bewilderment in every
moment.

O Soul, I am a tiny particle cut off from Your shining Sun.
Without you, why? Why, without you? You are the basis of
my being.

O my beloved King, You are my guide and the light of my
path,
O You, free from my submission, O You, beyond my
possibility.

Didn't I Tell You?

Didn't I tell you? Don't go anywhere: I am your intimate
    friend.
In this mirage of creation, I am the spring of your life.

If you go from Me in anger for a hundred thousand years,
at last you will come to Me, for I am your end and aim.

Didn't I tell you not to be pleased with the colors of
    temptation?
I am the sublime designer of your total contentment.

Didn't I tell you that I am the ocean and you are a fish?
Don't go to the dry shore, for I am the sea of your serenity.

Didn't I tell you not to go toward the snares as birds do?
Come to me! I am the strength of your wings and your feet.

Didn't I tell you that they would rob you and make you cold?
I am the source of your fire, your pulse, and your warmth.

Didn't I tell you that they will give you ugly traits?
You won't recall that I am the fountainhead of your
    attributes.

Didn't I tell you not to ask, *How are one's affairs organized?*
I am the supreme organizer beyond any why and how.

If you are the light in the heart, know the path leading
    Home,
and if your attributes are divine, then I am your Lord.

I Am Down

I have a bad temper, I am weary, please pardon me.
How could my temper be nice, my Beloved, without Your
    beautiful face?

Without You, I am like cold winter, torturing people.
When with You, I'm like a flower garden, and my temper is
    like spring.

Without You I have no wisdom. I'm vexed. Whatever I say is
    crooked.
I am embarrassed by my wisdom, and wisdom is shamed by
    the light of Your face.

What is the cure for stale water? It is to go back to the sea.
What is the cure for a bad temper? It is to see the Beloved.

I see the water of life is imprisoned in the quagmire of the
    body.
I dig out the soil to make my path leading to the sea.

You have an elixir that You give to Your hopeless ones,
    concealed,
so the hopeful do not cry out loud, begrudging it.

O heart, as long as you can, do not take your eyes off the
    Beloved,
even if He shies away or takes you to His side.

Mention the Name

Mention the name of the One whose beauty brings the dead
    person to life.
The weeping of the whole world turns into laughter through
    union with Him.

Remember the One when His goodness is revealed.
The goodness of the world is worthless before His.

Life-giving water is streaming under His throne.
Whoever drinks from this stream will live forever.

One night the Sun kissed the leg of His throne.
Now, the Sun shines over the firmament forever.

The lives of His lovers are all meek and humble.
Greedy dust was thrown under the feet for this reason.

The deer's navel took the aroma of musk from His tresses,
so the lion on hunt in the meadow began to roar.

When feather and wing of the lover's fantasy were burned by
    the fire of the heart,
like the Sun and the Moon, without feather and wing, it
    began to fly.

Happy is the soul who was bestowed the grace of Shams-e
    Tabriz.
It went beyond the nine heavens and dwelled in placelessness.

O Heart

O heart, sit before a person who knows all about heart.
Wend your way under the tree that bears fresh flowers.

In this herbalist market, do not roam around aimlessly.
Sit before that certain person who has sweets in his shop.

Since you do not have a measuring tool, everyone may take
    you in.
One may plate copper yellow, thinking he has real gold in his
    chest.

He will have you sit by the door, cleverly making you think
    he will come.
Don't sit waiting by the door: that place has two doors.

Wherever you see a cauldron boiling, don't bring your bowl,
for every boiling cauldron may hold something else.

Not every sugarcane has sugar, nor every descent, an ascent.
Not every eye contains meaning, nor every sea, pearls.

O you drunken, beautiful nightingale, lamenting more and
    more,
your song will have its effect even among the granite rocks
    and rocky cliffs.

Put down your head if it doesn't fit in the eye of the needle.
The thread won't pass through because of its knot.

This awakened heart is like a torch. Cover it up and hide it.
Let desire pass by, for it has much feverish anxiety and
    mischief.

When your passion subsides, you will settle in a spring.
You will be the companion of an intimate Friend with a
    serene heart.

When you have a tranquil heart, you become like a green tree
that keeps on giving fresh fruit—the journey is within the
    heart.

Over the Firmament

Over the firmament at dawn, my moon-faced Beloved
    appeared.
Descending from heaven, He became concerned about me.

Like a falcon who suddenly dives to take a bird as its prey,
the Beloved took me away and began turning the firmament
    around.

When I looked at myself, I couldn't see me,
because my body had become like a spirit by the Beloved's
    grace.

When I traveled in the spirit, I saw nothing but the Beloved,
until the secret of His manifestation at the beginning was
    fully revealed.

The nine heavens were totally sunk in the Beloved.
The ship of my whole being disappeared in that Sea.

A wave came forth on the surface and wisdom rose up,
and its eminence spread, becoming like this and like that.

The sea foamed and every piece of that foam
brought about designs here and shapes and figures there.

Every tiny particle of foam got its sign from the Sea,
and at times became present, floating on the current of the
Sea.

Without the fortune of being the obedient one of Shams al
Haqq of Tabriz,
one can neither see the Beloved nor become an everlasting
Sea.

Since I Saw Your Face

Since I saw Your face, O my bright moon and candle,
wherever I sit, I am happy and wherever I go, I'm in a flower
garden.

Wherever the thought of the Beloved comes, that is a
beautiful place.
In whatever state I may be in, a new joy springs to life.

If all the doors in this six-door Sufi house were closed,
the Beloved from placelessness would peek through from my
tiny chink.

He comes in with salutation, bringing forth hundreds of
sweets and spirits.
Being the King and the King of kings, He plays the Sepahan[24]
key.

I am the brightest Sun, I rend asunder all veils.
I am the new Spring, coming to remove all thorns.

For whoever wants joy and good times day and night,
I am the essence and joy of sweets and the life of fruit trees.

*I have a hard time hearing You. Please repeat Your words to
me.*
Describe it without weariness, for my head is slow and dull.

He says: *Those hard-hearing ears are far better than smart heads.*
This one has a hundred more merits. Here it is I, there, desires.

Now You are with me, the Fortune, the Essence of life and happiness.
You are the Heaven, the Beauty of paradise and beyond.

You are the Mountain, the Phoenix and the true Faith.
You are Water and the Water Giver, the Orchard, the Cypress and my Lily.

The firmament bows down its head. Lands of Earth put down their heads.
The heart says, *I am wax before You but hard as iron with others.*

Today the King Came

Today, when the King came in secret to pay a visit to the
    crazy ones,
all spiritually inspired crazy souls cried aloud to praise the
    King.

Among the loudest cries of all, the King recognized my
    voice,
for my voice has been cleansed of the animal breath.

The King said majestically, *This crazy one is breaking the
chain.*
If I am what You call crazy, You are the Solomon for
    madmen.

O King, You know the secrets of birds and You spellbind
    monsters.
Perhaps You may charm and enchant this crazy one, too.

An old man went before the King saying, *Put this man in
chains,*
for this crazy one has caused riots and turmoil in this place.

The King said, *This crazy one would tear apart any chain*
     but My tresses.
He will not accept any chains: You do not know his nature.

He will rend apart thousands of chains to fly toward Me.
He will become Everything That Returns to Me, for he is a
     trained falcon.

Coming Forth

Sprinkle the path, for the Beloved is coming forth.
Give good news to the orchard—the aroma of spring is
   coming.

Open the pathway for the full-moon Beloved.
From His light-bestowing face, light radiates forth.

The heavens are rent apart, the world's in turmoil.
The fragrance of ambergris and musk is rising. His majesty
   is coming forth!

The splendor of the Orchard, Fortune, is coming forth.
Sorrow disappears, for moonlike beauty is coming forth.

The arrow is released, it goes to the target.
Why are we sitting back? The King is on a hunt, coming
   forth.

The orchard greets Him, the cypress stands erect.
The low-lying greens are in motion, blossoms are riding
   high.

The denizens of heaven are drinking wine.
The spirit is stone-drunk, and the intellect languishes.

When you reach our district—silence is our nature,
for our talk brings forth contamination and dust.

Harmony

I will run fast to reach the riding horsemen.
I will cease to exist, cease to be, to come before the Soul of
  souls.

I've become joyous, joyous! I've become specks of fire.
I will burn down the house to reach the nowhere-land.

I will become dust to grow green from You.
I will become low water, crawling to reach the Garden.

Since I fell from heaven, I've become a fluttering particle.
I will be secure and stable when I reach the end.

Heaven is a place of dignity, Earth, a place of waste.
I will be freed from these dangers when I come before the
  King.

Unbelief and annihilation are the gems of earth and air.
I have come into the heart of infidelity to reach fidelity.

The balanced King of the Universe seeks but lovers in tune.
My face became like a golden coin to arrive at harmony.

The grace of God is like water: it flows only to low places.
I'll become like the earth, nothing—until I reach the
    Merciful One.

Without illness, no physician gives medicine.
I will be all pain until I reach the cure.

I Swear By You

Once again I'm frenzied, in such a state.
  I swear by You.
Every bond that You bind me with I'll tear apart.
  I swear by You.

I'm like the wheel of fate. I'm moon and candle by Your
    glow.
I'm all intellect, all love and soul.
  I swear by You.

My joy is from You. I languish from Your thorn.
Whatever direction You turn, I turn.
  I swear by You.

I was wrong. Being wrong in this state—no wonder
that at this moment I cannot tell wine and goblet apart.
  I swear by You.

I've become a madman that binds demons with bonds.
I know the language of birds. I'm Solomon.
  I swear by You.

I don't want this fleeting life—You are my dear life.
I don't want this soul full of sorrow—You are my soul.
  I swear by You.

Apart from love, if any other feeling arises in my heart,
I sweep it from its yard this very moment.
  I swear by You.

When you hide from me, I'm all darkness and infidelity,
and when You reappear, I'm a believer.
    I swear by You.

As I drink water from a jug, in it Your image I see.
If I take a breath without You, I'm all regret.
    I swear by You.

In heaven without You, I'm a gloomy, dark cloud.
In the flower garden without You—it's prison for me.
    I swear by You.

Sama[25] of my ears is Your name, *sama* of my intelligence,
        Your cup of wine.
I beg You to raise me up, for I am totally destroyed.
    I swear by You.

With love, I say that He is the lion and I, the deer.
What deer is this that guards the lions!
    I swear by You.

O come—You, who left me once! Whatever goes comes
        again.
You are not that—swear by me. I am not that—
    I swear by You.

O denier within my soul, don't deny in secret,
for I can read the secret of your fate.
    I swear by You.

From the love of Shams-e Tabriz, I'm awake all night,
like a particle floating round and round, distressed.
    I swear by You.[26]

Show Your Face

Show Your face. Don't veil it from me,
O You, like a moon in seven heavens notable.

I, among the lovers out of passion,
came from a trip on a long, long road.

O You, who possess within Your very being
hundreds of thousands of nymphs, palaces, and heavens,

look down from your heights toward
these crowds of lovesick lovers.

O Sufi Cupbearer, give us some wine,
not from the vat nor from the grapes,

such a wine whose intense aroma
pulls out the dead from their graves.

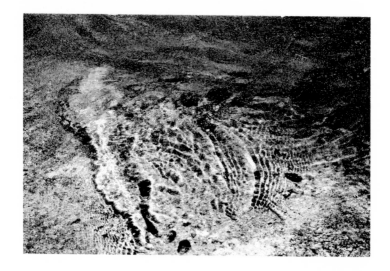

I Died a Hundred Times

I died a hundred times before I learned
that when Your aroma comes, I live again.

A hundred times, I gave up my life and soul.
I was born again when I heard Your voice.

When I saw Your face, I could no longer see myself.
You are my spring festival, I, your burnt-up incense stick.

I set up a trap in my inner self to hunt love again.
That Bird of prey took me away as a bird again.

The twirling fire is in the core of the lover's chest.
I am like a black sky circling Your moonlit face.

At that auspicious hour, You sealed Your pledge.
All my repentance broke away, and I was what I was.

My intellect blocked my path: *I'll take you to the King.*
So I followed my intellect and got nowhere.

The Beloved

O brother, I dreamt of my Beloved last night.
He was sleeping at the side of a spring among sweetbriars.

Nymphs and angels circled around Him hand over hand.
Tulip and jasmine gardens danced, side by side.

Wind was delicately moving His tresses to the side.
The aroma of musk and ambergris came from every curl.

Wind became intoxicated and stole the tresses from His face,
like a bright light with cover detached.

In the beginning of my dream I said, *Be quiet.*
Wait till I come to myself. Don't even breathe.

It's Harmful

It's harmful, it's harmful, it's harmful, harmful
to be sober among the selfless and the drunk ones.

O Cupbearer, bear no fear, keep pouring more wine
until no sane and sober remain in the world.

The Beloved is saying, *If you are in love, be crazy!*
The sober one is cold in the circle of the crazy ones.

If a sane one comes to you, say you are busy.
If a lover comes, take his hand and show him the way.

Finding faults comes from the weary intellect.
A thirsty one never sees faults in running water.

The denying intellect will never accept the signs.
Be a signless one so the sign will not be wounded.

Become like Joseph, even if the vain enslave you in the
    marketplace.
Become a flower garden, even if you may not be
    acknowledged.

Become like Jesus, even if you have no home.
Become His eyes, even if you have no clothes.

Two Rubai

Seek the knowledge that unties your knots.
Seek the knowledge before it's time to depart.

Leave behind nonexistence that appears to exist.
Seek the existence that nonexistent seems.

* * *

Dance is not to stand up from time to time
And swirl dust under your two feet.

Dance is being at *sama*—[27]
and losing the worlds of here and hereafter.

SA'DI

Flood of Nothingness

Once again, I am still drunk from last night's wine.
From the Garden of Union with the Soul of souls, I have
    flowers at my side.

If, happily drunk, with intense passion I stir up the world,
don't blame me, for I have burning desire for the Friend.

O Cupbearer, bring me a goblet of wine! I've repented for
    my piety.
O Minstrel, play a song, for I'm ashamed of my repentance.

Pour the flood of nonexistence into my whole being,
for I have dust on my heart from the clay of existence.

Zealously, I washed away anything bearing traces of my
    image,
for beautiful images and traces are dwelling in my heart.

I am Moses on the Mount Sinai of love, in the valley of
    yearning.
Those with hearts broken by *you cannot see Me*[28] are
    thousands like me.

You departed. My heart, my patience, and my knowledge
    went, too.
Come again! I have a little bit life left to sacrifice at Your
    feet.

How long will You twirl me like compasses around You?
I have become a vagrant, but my feet are steadfast.

One must have the Total Intellect to calm down the heart.
Where is the Intellect? Where is the Heart to settle me down?

From the wine that Your love poured into Sa'di's soul,
until the dawn of resurrection, he keeps yearning for You.

The Heights of Beauty

When You come, I need not to talk about myself,
and when You're standing, it's not polite not to fall.

If ever so delicately You walk through the garden gate,
the red rose is ashamed that it has bloomed at all.

When a flower reaches the heights of beauty, the nightingale
    grows restless.
Now everyone knows the heart's sorrow, which I'd
    concealed.

In hopes that You may have placed Your foot somewhere,
I swept all the dust of Shiraz with my eyes to find You.

In two, three dawns when the breeze brings forth the flowers'
    fragrance,
apart from my Mate, I will die more readily than the
    nightingale.

Have you not heard how Farhad[29] cut through the rock?
But I'm cutting a hole in Your threshold stone with my tears.

No wonder that all night long my eyes were open:
Thinking of You through the night, it is strange if I sleep.

Your faithful servants would spare a thousand lives of Sa'di.
You tell them to do it—and then say, *I didn't!*

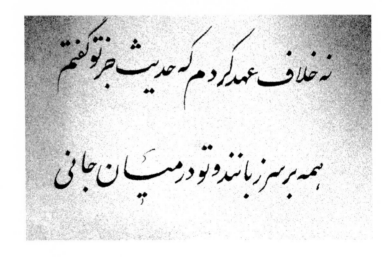

نه خلاف عهد کردم که حدیث جز تو گفتم

همه بر سر زبانند و تو در میان جانی

Like Dew

You came through the door and I went out of myself—
like going from this world into another.

My ears were on the path to hear news of the Friend.
The Possessor of news came, and I became newsless.

Like dewdrops I had fallen before the Sun.[30]
Love reached my soul, and I ended up in Capella.[31]

I said, *If I see Him, the pain of yearning will be calmed.*
I saw Him, and my yearning was intensified.

I did not have the strength to go to the Friend.
For a while I went by foot, and then I went by head.

To watch Him strolling, to hear Him talking,
from head to toe I became all hearing, all seeing.

How can I withdraw my eyes from Him,
since the first sight I saw in the beginning was He?[32]

I dislike Your loving-kindness any day, any time,
if as a result, I sit calm and happily content.

He did not care to hunt me as His prey.
I myself became ensnared in the bonds of His glance.

They say, *Sa'di, What made your rosy cheeks so yellow?*
The elixir of Love fell on my copper heart and turned it to
  gold.

Who Am I To Desire You?

Who am I to desire You to be mine? It is not fair
for You to be my Beloved nor for me to be Yours.

May You bestow some grace upon me,
for I lack substance to be equal to You.

I cannot justify myself to be one of Your friends,
for I see You as my flower and me as Your thorn.

I had never expected You to trap me in Your snare,
for I am not worthy to be ensnared by You.

I will never know the meaning of grief and happiness
until I cherish Your joy and suffer Your sorrows.

I cannot run away from my rivals to come before You,
but only when You scold and chastise me in Your presence.

If God finds me full of sins and guilt,
I need His grace, for I am only a tool.

O, the world's Qibla,[33] people love my eloquent speech,
for they see how much I love You and long for You.

I do not deserve to desire You nor to know You.
It is only through Your mercy that I come closer to You.

Although I know union with You is beyond my reach,
I'd rather die than cease seeking You.

Not only in this world but in the world of hereafter
will I remain steadfastly loyal and faithful to You.

If You don't approve of Sa'di, then dust be on him,
for You are my glory and I am Your shame.

BIOGRAPHIES
OF THE POETS

Dr. Javad Nurbakhsh

(1926–2008)

Dr. Javad Nurbakhsh was born in Kerman, Iran, in 1926. Dr. Nurbakhsh was initiated into the Ni'matullahi Sufi Order at age 16. At age 20 he was appointed by his Master, Munis Ali Shah, to the position of sheikh (spiritual director), and after Munis Ali Shah passed way, he became the Master of the Ni'matullahi Sufi Order. He was then 26 years old.

Dr. Nurbakhsh attended medical school at the University of Tehran and received his medical doctor's diploma in 1952. In 1962, he was invited to undertake postgraduate studies at the Sorbonne University in Paris. He then returned to Tehran, where he completed his studies in psychiatry. He later became Professor and Head of the Department of Psychiatry at Tehran University until his retirement in 1977.

Dr. Nurbakhsh was the author of over 80 works, including articles and other writings on psychiatry. However, his greatest contribution has consisted of books on various aspects of Sufism and the Sufi path. Many of these works have been translated into English, including *Sufi Symbolism: The Nurbakhsh Encyclopedia of Sufi Terminology*, a monumental and unique 16-volume compendium of the terms used by Sufis in their writings over the centuries; *Divane Nurbakhsh*, a collection of poetry of love and loving; *The Path: Sufi Practice*, a book of essays that provides perhaps the most accurate and complete account of the practice and theoretical basis of Sufism in English today; *The Psychology of Sufism*, an in-depth study of the *nafs* (ego) from the Sufi point of view.

Dr. Nurbakhsh also edited and published many important Sufi texts, in particular the poetry and essays of Shah

Ni'matullah, as well as the poetical works by Ansari, Ahmad Ghazali, Ruzbihan Baqli, 'Iraqi, and Shabistari.

Dr. Nurbakhsh holds a place of great distinction and influence in the history of Sufism as a direct result of his efforts to revive the works of great Sufi Masters of the past (Hallaj, Shibli, Jonaid, Kharaqani, and Bayazid), many of whom had been long forgotten.

Hafez

Shams ud-Din Muhamad Hafez Shirazi

(c. 1320–c. 1389)

Hafez was born around the year 1320 in Shiraz, Iran. Not much credible information is known about his early years, but according to tradition, it is said that he had memorized the Koran by listening to his father's recitations of it. He also had memorized many works of Sa'di, Attar, Rumi, and others. He spent almost his entire life in Shiraz.

Hafez is Iran's most beloved poet. Scholars conclude that he composed approximately 5,000 poems, of which some 500-700 have been preserved. His *Divan* is recognized as a classical work of Persian Sufi literature. The Western world learned to know about Hafez largely through Wolfgang Goethe and, later, Ralph Waldo Emerson. Other Western authors, such as Nietzsche, Pushkin, Turgenev, Carlyle, and Garcia Lorca, have also been admirers of Hafez.

Hafez displayed great dexterity in his use of words, combining them in original ways and even inventing new ones, which since his time have become a part of the Persian language and literary tradition. His poetry spanned many subjects, including Divine Love, fate and fortune, human love, youth and old age, hypocrisy and sincerity, greed and generosity, God-intoxication, jealousy, friendship, the emptiness of material wealth and power, the beauty of the Perfect Masters, the desperate yearning for the Beloved, and the ecstasy of Divine Union.

Shah Ni'matullah

Shah Ni'matullah Wali

(c. 1330–c. 1431)

Shah Ni'matullah Wali was born c. 1330 in Aleppo, Syria. His father's side of the family included many scholars of Arabic culture; his mother's side hailed from Shiraz, Iran. Before entering the path of Sufism, he studied with a number of various scholars of his time such as Shah Rokn ud-Din Shirazi and Sheikh Shams ud-Din Makki. He studied the works of many great philosophers, among them Avicenna and Ibn Arabi. However, learning exoteric knowledge did not quench his thirst for the truth, for it did not satisfy his inner longing.

Shah Ni'matullah continued searching for a spiritual Master. Whenever he heard of one, he sought him out, but none could quench his thirst, until in a mosque in Mecca he met Sheikh Abdullah Yafei. From his first glance at Sheikh Abdullah, Shah Ni'matullah saw himself a mere drop of water before the ocean. Becoming his disciple, Shah Ni'matullah served his Master for seven years and through him reached the highest spiritual perfection; the disciple became a Master.

Shah Ni'matullah inspired thousands to enter the path of Sufism. It is said that he was extremely serene and dignified, easily attracting people to himself. Shah Ni'matullah believed that everyone is capable of entering the Sufi path, so those who were dismissed by other Masters, Shah Ni'matullah used to guide and bring onto the path of God.

It is believed that Shah Ni'matullah lived to be 100 years old. He wrote 1,550 *ghazals*,[1] 39 *masnavi*,[2] 294 *rubai*, and 131 discourses. The Unity of Being was a key principle of Shah Ni'matullah's teaching and writing.[3]

Shah Ni'matullah was the founder of the Ni'matullahi Sufi Order.

---

[1] *Ghazal*: love poem.

[2] *Masnavi*: a work in rhymed couplets.

[3] The poems translated here are based on the original Persian text as corrected and published by Dr. Javad Nurbakhsh, *Divan-e Shah Ni'matullah Wali* (Tehran: Khaniqahi Ni'matullahi, 1967).

Rumi

Maulana Jalal ud-Din Rumi

(1207–1273)

Rumi was born in 1207 into the family of a renowned theologian and scientist in the region known as Afghanistan today, which in Rumi's day was part of the Persian Empire. When the invading Mongols threatened to conquer his place of birth, his family moved to Konya, Turkey, the location of Rumi's mausoleum.

At the early age of 24, Rumi inherited the work and mission of his famous father. By the age of 36, he had become a respected theologian in Konya, with thousands of followers. Enthralled by his own talents and the veneration he received from others, he could easily have remained in the position of a successful teacher and not continued further on his own spiritual path. But then he met his master Shams-e Tabriz, who in the course of three years transformed him into a fervent lover of God.

Rumi's work reaches across religious and social boundaries. As he says in one of his poems, "I'm not a Christian or a Jew or a Zoroastrian, not even a Muslim . . . I'm not from India or China or Bulgaria ... My place is placelessness." It is said that his funeral was attended by Muslims, Jews, Persians, Christians, and Greeks.

Rumi's most famous works are his *Masnavi*, in seven volumes, and his massive *Divan-e Shams*, comprising thousands of verses in praise of his spiritual teacher Shams. He also was the author of a discourse in prose.

Sa'di

Mosleh ud-Din Sa'di Shirazi

(c. 1203–c. 1291)

The year of Sa'di's birth is not precisely known, but many scholars agree that it was around 1203; according to other sources he was born in 1184 and lived until about 1291. Having begun his life in Shiraz, he lived a colorful life and experienced much: he studied widely, traveled extensively, and wrote poetry and prose.

The American writer Ralph Waldo Emerson (1803–1882) in his 180-line poem, "Saadi," dedicated to him, describes the ancient poet as a rare wonder among poets. He says that those chosen few have been gifted by God with a lyre upon which to play their songs; then he adds, "Many may come, / But one shall sing ...Though there come a million / Wise Saadi dwells alone."

The best-known works of Sa'di are his *Bustan* (*Fruit Orchard*) and *Gulestan* (*Rose Garden*). His works reflect his own experiences, as he expounds on questions of social behavior that touch various areas of life. To this day, *Gulestan* is one of the most popular books in Persian-speaking countries. Many of Sa'di's poems reveal deep inner experiences and yearning for God.

A famous poem by Sa'di talks about the kinship of all humankind, beginning with the words "Of one Essence is the human race..." Sa'di's verse graces the entrance to the Hall of Nations of the United Nations building in New York.

NOTES

Sufi Symbolism[4]

To express the intense longing of the heart, Sufi poetry makes use of numerous metaphors and allusions; however, some of them may not readily reveal the meaning of the content. In Sufi poetry, understanding a poem requires nearness to God, and no shortcuts exist for applying the meaning of a term to understand the poem. The brief glossary provided below offers authentic definitions that are faithful to the tradition of Sufism, but those definitions are not necessary for unlocking the meaning of the poems. And some Sufi poems contain content that is beyond comprehension at the usual level of understanding.

The partial glossary below is a general list, and all definitions may not apply to the use of these terms in the current collection of poems. Also, not every instance of a word, for example, *foot* or *eyebrow*, is used with the identical meaning. It is also worth noting that in the Sufi tradition the word *Master* is used to describe a human being perfected in God, a person who is the most highly evolved. For that reason it is capitalized in this book.

Beloved or *Friend:* God, in that He is the only one worthy of friendship from any point of view.

---

[4] The explanations of symbolism are based on the definitions provided in: Dr. Javad Nurbakhsh, *Sufi Symbolism: The Nurbakhsh Encyclopedia of Sufi Terminology (Farhang-e Nurbakhsh),* in 16 volumes (London and New York: Khaniqahi-Nimatullahi Publications, 1984-2004). *Sufi Symbolism* is available at all the Khaniqahi Nimatullahi centers around the world. For a complete catalog of Sufi symbolism, the reader can refer to this series of books.

Cupbearer (Saqi): The Absolute Beloved as well as the Master of the Sufi path and the giver of grace who dispenses the wine of love to His lovers.

Cypress: A much loved and adored tree in Persia, used in Sufi poetry to symbolize the beauty and noble stature of the Beloved; may symbolize Truth; may also signify the Figure of the Beloved (see Figure).

Ecstasy: Infusion of God into the Sufi's heart, which is experienced sometimes as joy, sometimes as sadness.

Eye: Attribute of Divine, Absolute Insight; also said to signify Divine Beauty.

Eyebrow (the curve of the eyebrow): Represents the subtleties and delicate aspects of the attributes of Divine Beauty.

Eyes, bewitching: Alludes to God's withholding of the knowledge of the truth of things from the wayfarer, in order for him to come to rely more on his or her own efforts.

Face: The mirror of theophanies (God's manifestations or appearances).

Face, radiant: The theophanies (God's appearances) of beauty.

Figure: The quality of worshipfulness, which belongs to God alone.

Foot: The Divine Attribute of comprehension, the attention and spiritual attraction exerted by the Beloved, the loving kindness emanating from the Beloved; Divine Will.

Hand: The Divine Attribute of power.

Head: The Divine Attribute of will.

Master of the Tavern of Ruin: Alludes to the Beloved, and also to the Perfect Master capable of perfecting others.

Moth: The sacrifice of one's life to the Beloved, just as a moth sacrifices its life in the flame around which it has been circling.

Ringlet (or curl) of tresses: The difficulties in the world of multiplicity, which cause particular anguish for the beginner on the path.

Shoulder: The Divine Attribute of glory.

Simurgh: A mythological bird. The Perfect Man, the wayfarer who is in Union, one who has gnosis of Divine Essence.

Step: The Divine Attribute of comprehensiveness.

Tavern: The heart of the perfect Sufi; the Master who has realized union with God; also can symbolize the house of the Sufi Master (*khaniqah*), where Sufis gather.

Over the years, the Sufis have used this kind of mystical terminology as a "means for describing the Beloved while protecting the secrets of their inward journey and outward manner....Such images and metaphors penetrate the mind more readily and are impressed upon the heart more profoundly than direct speech."[5]

[5] Dr. Javad Nurbakhsh, *What the Sufis Say* (New York: Khaniqahi-Nimatullahi Publications, 1980), p. 48.

Notes to Poems

1. Crazy, from Persian *divaneh*: Being crazy, crazed with love of God, a term often used in Sufi poetry.

2. Master of the Holy Fire: Perfected human being who is living in the current age, who possesses all the divine attributes, the Solomon of his time.

3. *Rendan* (pl.), from *rend* (sing.): A spiritually evolved, yet humble, individual whose true state is not revealed to anyone and who lives an ordinary life.

4. *Khaniqah*: House of the Sufis, where Sufis gather.

5. *Rendi*, from *rend*: A spiritually evolved, yet humble, individual whose true state is not revealed to anyone and who lives an ordinary life.

6. Crazy, from Persian *divaneh*: Being crazy, crazed with love of God, a term often used in Sufi poetry.

7. Sheikh: A disciple of a Perfect Master who is assigned to guide others to God; a teacher commissioned by the Perfect Master.

8. Jamshid's goblet: In old Persian mythology, King Jamshid had a goblet in which he could see the whole world.

9. *Saqi*: The Cupbearer, the Absolute Beloved as well as the Master of the Sufi path and the giver of grace who dispenses

the wine of love to His lovers; the One who bestows light and grace.

10. King Jam: A legendary king of Persia.

11. Kay: A legendary king of Persia.

12. King Jam and Kavous: Two legendary Persian kings.

13. Tooran king: A famous king in *Shahnameh Ferdoussi*, a long epic poem.

14. Shoaib: One of the Biblical prophets.

15. Khosro: A famous king of ancient Iran.

16. *Rend* (pl., *rendan*): See note 3.

17. Ni'matullah: The blessing of Allah (God); also the name of a Sufi master (Shah Ni'matullah).

18. *Rend*: See note 3.

19. Both worlds: This life and the afterlife.

20. *Rendan* (pl.), from *rend* (sing.): See note 3.

21. See note 17.

22. *Goblet of Jam*: A world-seeing goblet in old Persian mythology.

23. See note 17.

24. *Sepahan*: A musical key or scale in Persian music.

25. *Sama*: Literally, "hearing"—listening with the ear of the heart to music, while being in a special state where no vestige

of self is left in one's awareness.

26. This ghazal (love poem) exists in two versions, both of which have been combined here into one ghazal, with some lines omitted.

27. *Sama*: Literally, "hearing"—listening with the ear of the heart to music, while being in a special state where no vestige of self is left in one's awareness.

28. *You cannot see Me*: Refers to what God said to Moses on Mt. Sinai, Exodus 33:20: "But He said, 'You cannot see Me. A man cannot have a vision of Me and still exist.'" Koran 7:143: "The Lord said, 'You cannot see Me when I manifest My glory.'"

29. Farhad: Refers to the love story of Farhad and Shirin. In love with Shirin, Farhad cut a path to Shirin through the mountains to reach her palace.

30. Sun: In Persian, the name of Rumi's Master, Shams, means "Sun."

31. Capella: A massive star, the sixth brightest star in the night sky. Although it appears as one star, it actually consists of a pair of stars.

32. *Since the first sight I saw in the beginning was He*: Alludes to Koran 7:172: "God called the future descendants to come from the loins of the not-yet-created Adam and addressed them with the words: 'Am I not your Lord?', and they answered: 'Yes, we bear witness.'"

33. Qibla: In Islam, the direction that one should face during prayer.